I SPY
BACKYARD BUGS

Artworks from:
Freepik.com
Creativefabrica.com or licensed for commercial use.

For Further Communication:
Email: azulancreatives@gmail.com
Facebook: fb.com/azulancreatives
Website: www.azulancreatives.com

This Book Belongs To

_____

_____

_____

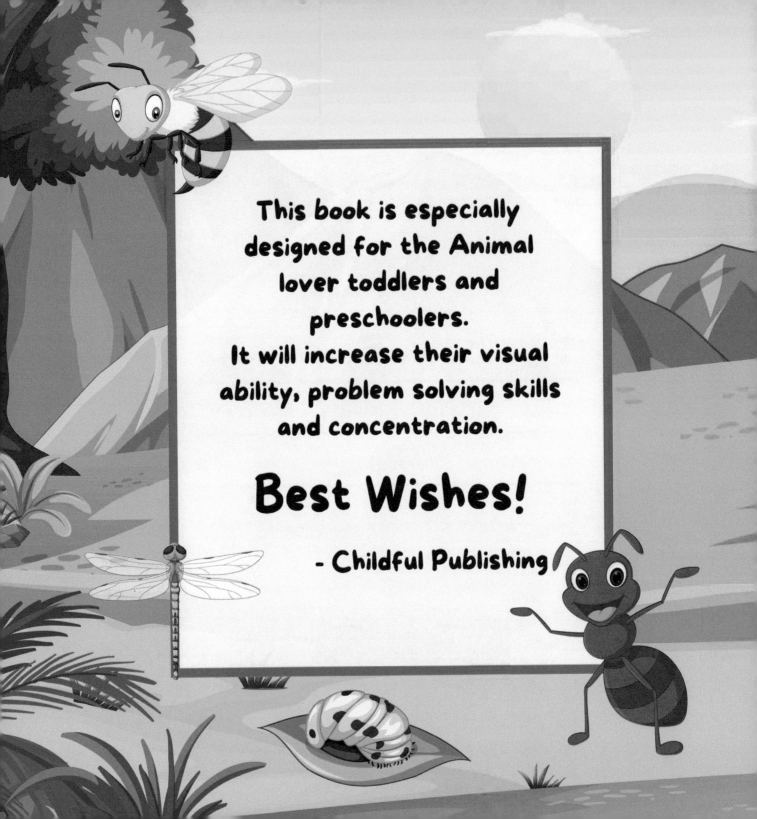

This book is especially designed for the Animal lover toddlers and preschoolers.
It will increase their visual ability, problem solving skills and concentration.

Best Wishes!

- Childful Publishing

I SPY with my little eye something beginning with...

A AND B

A is for

Ant

B is for

Butterfly

I SPY with my little eye something beginning with...

C AND D

C is for Cockroach

D is for Dragonfly

I SPY with my little eye something beginning with...

E AND F

E is for

Earwigs

F is for

Fly

I SPY with my little eye something beginning with...

G AND H

G is for

Grasshopper

H is for

Hymenoptera

I SPY with my little eye something beginning with...

I AND J

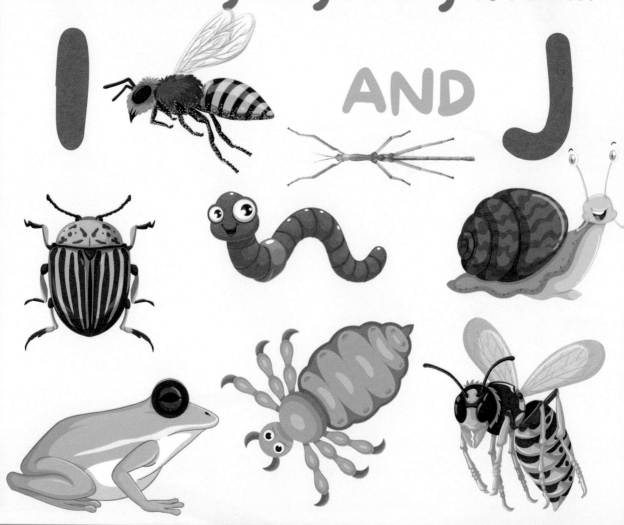

I is for

Indian Hornet

J is for

Jewel wasp

I SPY with my little eye something beginning with...

K AND L

K _{is for}

Katydids

L _{is for}

Louse

I SPY with my little eye something beginning with...

M AND N

M is for Mosquito

N is for Neuroptera

I SPY with my little eye something beginning with...

O AND P

O is for

Odonata

P is for

Proturans

I SPY with my little eye something beginning with...

Q AND R

Q is for

Queen Alexandra's Birdwing

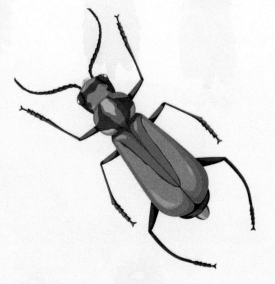

R is for

Raphidioptera

I SPY with my little eye something beginning with...

S AND T

S is for Snail

T is for Termite

I SPY with my little eye something beginning with...

U is for

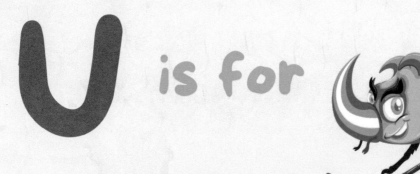

Unlined Giant Chafer

V is for

Venomous spider

I SPY with my little eye something beginning with...

W

AND X

W is for

Worm

X is for

Xerces Blue Butterfly

I SPY with my little eye something beginning with...

Y

AND Z

Y is for

Yellow Ants

Z is for

Zoraptera

I Spy 5 Missing Bugs

I Spied 5 Missing Bugs

I Spy Bug in Red

I Spied Bug in Red

I Spy Bug in Blue

I Spied Bug in Blue

I Spy Bug in Green

I Spied Bug in Green

I Spy Bug in Yellow

I Spied Bug in Yellow